Investment Attitude

5 biases
that keep us from
being rich

Law Steeple, MBA
Warren Buffett's Investment Strategy

IAN Books

An IAN Books paperback

Published by
IAN Books
41 Watchung Plaza, B242
Montclair, NJ 07042

Copyright © 2016 IAN Books

Cover photo: Chappellet Winery by Alex Hendricks

Special sales for educational use by nonprofits.
IANBooksEditor@yahoo.com

1. Investments. 2. Investment Strategies.
I. Steeple, Law 1948-. II. Title.

332.6--dc22
ISBN-13: 978-1533424518
ISBN-10: 1533424519
Library of Congress Control Number: 2016943143

IAN Books at Amazon.com

Wealth Without Wall Street:
Buy Direct -- Avoid the Commissions, Fees, Loads

The Insiders' Guides to Buying Discount Financial Services:
Buy Direct and Save $3,000 Every Year

Drop Your Insurance:
Buy Only What You Need

Create Financial Freedom Using Your Wealth Reserve™:
Fix your financial life

The Simple Financial Life:
How to get what you want without going into debt and living
paycheck to paycheck

Build Wealth Without Extra Money or Time:
You don't need to budget or get an extra job

Leah's Money Book:
"I want to control my own money."

The Working Millionaire:
$2,000,000 Tax-FREE Wealth Reserve ™ Self-insure Self-fund

Build Your Own $2,000,000 Tax-FREE Wealth Reserve™:
Self-insure Self-fund your lifestyle

Stop wasting $3,000 every year:
101
financial products **NOT** to buy and why

Wealth:
What every high school graduate needs to know in the 21st century

Contents

Biases keep us from being rich

The average investor earned just <u>3.79%</u> annually while the market index earned 11% over the last 30 years.
<u>http://www.dalbar.com/Portals/dalbar/cache/News/PressReleases/DALBAR %20Pinpoints%20Investor%20Pain%202015.pdf</u>

Why?

Despite overwhelming evidence that a stock market index fund beat 90% of stock pickers, most investors act as if they are successful Wall Street gurus. In one study, investors were asked about their acumen. "<u>Nearly two-thirds rated their financial sophistication as advanced</u>." Yet their test scores showed most failed financial literacy.

Are we born overconfident? Optimism is a wonderful trait we all prize in ourselves and loved ones. Life would be impossible without it. But for financial decisions, <u>overconfidence makes bad decisions worse</u>. When we don't sell a loser early (sunk cost fallacy), we tend to remember a better outcome than reality (hindsight bias). We don't learn from our mistakes. We continue in our beliefs because we find justifications (confirmation bias). We don't blame ourselves (attribution bias). We even make up a different history for some investments so we "win." We live in <u>Wobegon</u> where "all the children are above average."

We make judgments under uncertainty every day. I rush to get in front of the car next to me before I hit the 'closed lane' sign. I will crash if I misjudge car speed or distance. Usually I make it. But with stocks, *we think we know* about the future "price and growth" of that particular stock. But I can't control price or growth. I'm really gambling. I feel lucky: "I have to be in it to win it."

We may decide to buy a stock because it resembles the good one we remember we had in the past. So beginners' luck becomes a bias. If I was lucky before, this decision 'feels' the same based on my recreated history. (I enhanced the outcome to punch up my self-esteem.) *I must be a born genius*! My view of my status is enhanced every time I tell the story at parties or I hear another "genius" tell of his stock successes. At my job there are many "genius" stock pickers. I ignore the fact that if I wait long enough most stocks rise in value: there are many more winners than losers. Any monkey can pick winners with darts.

Without realizing it, I was dragged into buying a security because I was told that everyone else (herding bias) was buying it. Another time, I thought I was smart buying a value stock that had dropped from $90 to $50 (anchor bias). I sold in 1987 because I thought of more declines (base rate bias) after the first round.

So how did I finally control my biases. My experiences as a speculator/gambler ended when I got to observe the Street's operations first hand. I read about my biases and the research on stock-picking vs index success. I read about Buffett, Bogle and other non-commissioned experts. I lost money on single stocks.

I learned to ignore the stories of "success" in the press. Good stories sell Wall Street products. The public is told we *must* pay for good performance. Other Wall Street stories include the myths of buy low, sell high; manager tenure; proven performer; get in on the ground floor; concentrate portfolio, value investing.

Stories help us visualize ourselves as financial heros. However, that facts are most investors earn 3.79%. Listen to the real expert: Warren Buffett says "use low-cost index funds":

"A very low-cost index is going to beat a majority of the amateur-managed money or professionally-managed money."

Mr Buffett said that his secret is compound interest not trading:

My wealth has come from a combination of living in America, some lucky genes, and **compound interest**.

Compounding high investment returns is money earning money on its *prior* earnings over time. Simple but powerful.

The only way to compound our money is to **leave it alone** and pay NO taxes and LOW costs. Our stock market index fund can then compound at 10-12% per year over time. The average investor earned JUST 3.79% instead of 11%.

Forget Wall Street. Use the non-profit investment companies to earn higher returns. According to an unbiased

<u>Morningstar</u> study, low-cost funds beat high-cost funds all the time. <u>amazon.com/Everything-Youve-Heard-About-Investing-is-Wrong/dp/0812928393</u>

When we invest $250 a month, $3,000 a year, in successful businesses at low cost, we earn more than any other investment. After 10 years, we have about $50,000—more than the $30,000 we paid because the businesses paid dividends and the businesses are worth more. Each year dividends add up. See chart below. After 20 years, we could have over $200,000 and after 35 years, over $1,000,000. Over time, the stocks of growing businesses are the **safest investment**. Stocks beat inflation.

Monthly Accumulation at 12% per year									
	5	10	15	20	25	30	35	40	45	50
$100	$8,167	$23,004	$49,958	$98,925	$187,884	$349,496	$643,095	$1,176,477	$2,145,469	$3,905,834
$200	$16,334	$46,008	$99,916	$197,850	$375,768	$698,992	$1,286,190	$2,352,954	$4,290,938	$7,811,668
$300	$24,501	$69,012	$149,874	$296,775	$563,652	$1,048,488	$1,929,285	$3,529,431	$6,436,408	$11,717,502
$500	$40,835	$115,020	$249,790	$494,625	$939,420	$1,747,480	$3,215,475	$5,882,385	$10,727,346	$19,529,169

Compounding works best when we put our money to work in successful businesses with *no income taxes* and *no broker fees.* Market returns of 12% are **possible but not guaranteed**. But, wouldn't you rather have $1 million or more rather than $215,000 after 35 years? Investing is all about putting your money in businesses so that in the future you can get back your money multiplied many times over. It is a calculated risk—a risk many wealthy people take because it works—it builds wealth.

The risk: $9 a day you give up for a 99% chance of receiving $1,000,000 or more in the future? Our experiences in life have no equivalent to this risk for most of us. But analyze the risk. You invest in a number of successful businesses. If one fails, you still earn 10-12% a year over time. Your account compounds at the full 10-12%. You pay no taxes as your money grows. You contribute a fixed amount like $250 a month (about $9 a day) for each of you automatically so you don't forget to send a check. You can budget it. You invest at little or no charge. Cost is the best predictor of success: Low-cost beats high-cost every time.

If you pay 2-3% to earn 10-12% you give up over a THIRD of your earnings. Your money does all the work if you leave it alone. You pay no taxes by using *a tax-FREE account.* ALL of your earnings are reinvested for the next period. The chart below illustrates tax-FREE compounding over time.

Fortunately, low-cost mutual funds and a tax-FREE trust were invented in the last few years. You can now avoid Wall Street's fees of 2-3% and income taxes FOREVER. Following certain simple steps, you can benefit from the FULL miracle of compounding **as Buffett does**. Many people like you have taken the steps to become wealthy over time. And now the steps have been made easier to execute. You can do it yourself in about an hour, online or on the phone. For most working people, building a $1,000,000 fund takes patience and time. They become wealthy by living below their means and investing in their own business or the businesses owned by the mutual funds they buy every month.

Tax-FREE v Taxable

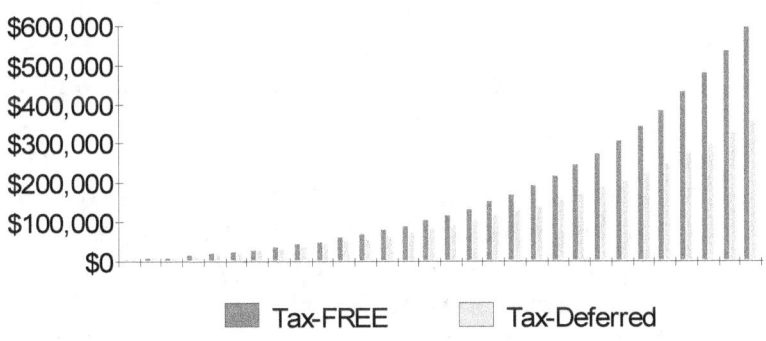

I have been in financial services for over 25 years. I ran sales organizations in several financial firms. I was a regular presenter at trade group conferences. I served on a number of state financial organizations. Working directly and indirectly with clients was my career. The wealthy don't get there by accident.

The key factor in building wealth is **maximizing the miracle of compounding**. You need to grow your wealth in a tax-FREE account, paying low fees. I will show how to use an IRS tax haven that can provide a tax-advantaged income source all your life. If you use this account correctly, the **tax-FREE** status is worth over $300,000 extra to you. Taxes are the greatest killer of wealth. This account, called a "**Wealth Reserve**™" by my colleague, Dan Keppel, grows without taxation as it accumulates. Unlike a regular account, you don't pay taxes every year on the dividends or value your account earns. When you let your balance compound, you can reach all your goals. See page 34. You can do this because you invest in a proven long-term investment—shares of growing companies worldwide via your fund shares.

After you accumulate a sizable balance—say $150,000— you can borrow from it to buy things like appliances and new used cars. You pay cash and avoid paying interest to a bank. You can also use it to cover your insurance deductibles and save policy premiums. Of course larger risks are covered by your regular high-deductible policies. You borrow deposits without tax or penalty.

The **miracle of compounding** works best if you use a mutual fund account at the lowest cost you can find. I show how to set up a low-cost "**Wealth Reserve**™" at no cost. I show you how to pick low-cost investments for long-term growth. You don't need to pay a broker or sales person to decide which securities to buy. Frankly, their fees can rob you of *63%* of your nest egg. PBS.org

Another benefit of the low-cost account is that it allows you to make equal contributions monthly. This is called "dollar cost averaging." It is convenient to invest the same amount monthly. If you and your spouse contribute $250 a month, your family could have $1,000,000 in less time. By investing a fixed amount each month, you buy shares at the least cost possible. You buy more shares when the price is low and less when it is high.

If your investing is done automatically, you have a better chance of success. **Automatic investing** makes investing a habit. The habit is actually another factor in building wealth. You can't miss making a contribution because you forget about the money coming out of your bank account. The people who succeed at building wealth are those who NEVER stop saving and investing.

You may be thinking this account sounds like your 401k or pension account at work. You are right. Your 401k or 403b works just like a **Wealth Reserve**™ except you *never* have to pay taxes on the accumulations. Most employer-sponsored plans are tax-*deferred*. You pay tax later. The difference can be over $400,000. You will have more to spend when you take the money out. Unlike a pension account, you don't need to take distributions until you want to. It is better than an annuity as a legacy for your heirs too. Heirs don't have to pay your income taxes after you're gone.

The **Wealth Reserve**™ may be the best way to accumulate wealth if your employer does not match your deposits. However, you can contribute much more to a 401k than a **Wealth Reserve**™ – up to $18,000 (2016) versus $5,500. Both accounts will compound earnings. One will be **tax-FREE** now AND later, in retirement. You can do both accounts—contributions grow without taxes for years. It is best to start with a **Wealth Reserve**™ which has a limit of $5,500. It may provide higher long-term accumulations than a 401k because there is zero, $0 tax on gains, ever.

Unlike other methods of investing for the future, a **Wealth Reserve**™ can provide a lifetime of tax-FREE growth. This is a powerful strategy! It uses the most powerful financial force available—**compounding** of high earnings over time. It avoids the greatest **killer** of wealth-building—TAXES. You pay no taxes on the accumulations and no taxes on the withdrawals later. And you don't pay broker or advisor fees every year either.

Here is a plan to help you avoid biases that keep you from being rich. You invest in high-earning securities over a period of time. You let compounding work its miracle over time. You pay $100,000 for $1,000,000 over time. You don't stop investing when the market goes up or down over time. As Warren Buffett said, "My wealth has come from a combination of living in America, some lucky genes, and **compound interest**."

1. Create a tax-FREE low-cost account without an advisor.
2. Set up tax-favored lifetime investment plan.
3. Compound high earnings over time.
4. Make monthly contributions automatic.
5. Use 10 low-cost diversified mutual funds.
6. Use stocks of growing companies worldwide.
7. Spend less than you make.
8. Buy financial products at a discount and save $3,000 a year.
9. Manage the account only once a year.
10. Take $80,000 tax-FREE income each year in retirement.

Building a low-cost account requires **patience**. If you are self-employed, you understand that it takes time to build a business. You have to have the right product and then find the customers that enable you to earn a living and profit to expand.

If you work for others, you don't have to be a genius to become financially independent. Wealthy people control their spending by various methods. Some have goals and budgets that help them build their spending and investing habits. Some are thrifty or don't spend more than they make. They all invest regularly.

Wealthy people have learned that there is no quick way to become wealthy. They let the **miracle of compounding** work. They don't pay high taxes or fees. They learn and avoid biases.

It does not take a lot of time to manage your account. In fact, it takes only an hour to set up a **Wealth Reserve**™ and takes only 1 hour per year to manage it. As master investor Warren Buffett said:

We continue to make more money when *snoring* than when active.
Berkshirehathaway.com

Building wealth is more about NOT doing something with your investments. Activity in investing usually is the result of fear or greed. Activity usually costs more than the gains.

People with assets cultivate **patience**. They don't panic when their account goes down. In fact, they buy more assets when others are selling. They know they cannot build a small fortune overnight with a quick buy and sell strategy. Patience allows assets to "grow by themselves." Wealthy people buy assets that grow— earnings on earnings, interest on interest. Note on page 24 that Tom's account kept growing even after falling some years. The client never lost money because he did NOT sell in down years!

People with assets understand that to build wealth they need to keep their money working. They do this by buying only the products they need. In fact, that has become their way of life. For instance, they can afford to buy an expensive new car but they don't. They know that new cars lose value quickly. The money they save adds to their wealth so they can reach their goals quicker. They invest in the businesses they own or in the securities of successful companies. They improve their future by buying more assets that "grow by themselves." The chart on page 34 illustrates annual stock market growth since 1950.

Wealthy people know about the **miracle of compounding and low-cost investing**. If we invest $250 per spouse, we may have $1 million in 28 years, $2 million in 35 years. $250 a month is only $9 a day. That $9 a day is building our future life. It provides more security than insurance. In a sense, having assets is the best insurance we can have.

All it takes is the Buffett *Investment Attitude* and time.

1

$1,000,000 tax-FREE

Building a $1 million tax-FREE low-cost account takes time. If we own a business, it would take a lifetime. We would have to find and sell the right product to the right customer in a profitable manner. It is difficult to build a successful business like Amazon or Apple has done. If we are lucky, we could buyout our boss after working at a skilled trade for years. Many wealthy people have followed this path. They are ***The Working Millionaires***.

Another way to build wealth is to take some of our salary from working for others and invest it. We can accumulate $1,000,000 over time, depending on the type of investments we make. Using a brokerage account, it takes about 72 years. Using a low-cost stock index account, it takes about 33 years.

We can understand how this can happen from DALBAR's findings of the average managed account returns of just 3.79%. Time is the key to accumulating wealth. http://www.saferchild.org/power/ Wealthy people typically hold, not trade, many types of investments. To become wealthy, we must start with a mutual fund that holds all types of investments. Our investment of $250 a month can go to the one low-cost fund that owns all types of investments—a stock index fund.

If we are going to accumulate $1,000,000 in about 33 years, we need to find investments that can earn 10% to 12% a year, year after year. We need to understand reward and risk. If we want to have a balance of $1 million, we would have to wait 72 years for our $250 a month to grow in a "managed" account at 3.79%. Brokerage accounts are designed to maximize the returns of the brokers and firm owners. The high costs support the Wall Street lifestyle. The managed account fees take up to 63% of our total possible accumulations over time. They are not for long-term investing. They are for short-term gambling.

Investing in low-cost stock funds provide almost the reverse risk profile. Historically, the value of a stock market index

—a bunch of stocks—has varied greatly in any one year. However, over time, the value has ALWAYS increased. This is the reason wealthy people have most of their money in the stocks of growing companies.

Remember, we are looking for an investment that compounds our money at 10-12% year after year. The reward and risk profile of owning a bunch of stocks is like owning a business —in any one year, we might have a loss or we might gain. But over time we have more gains than losses and thus succeed.

Range of annual returns of stocks, 1950 – 2000

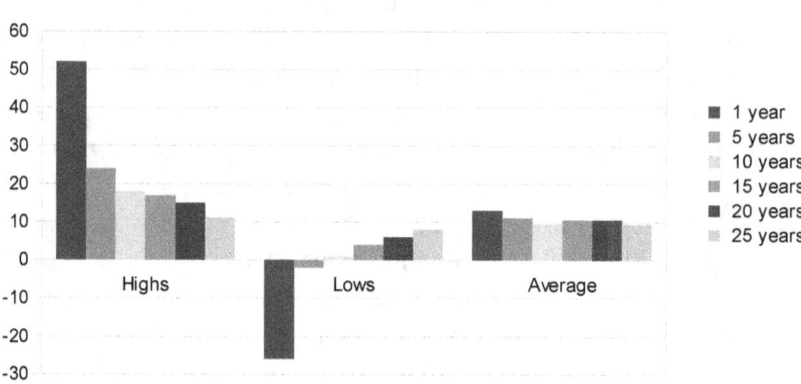

Bank savings are a great place to park our money for a year in case we need it to repair our car, appliances or house. However, bank savings are not really an investment. People who put all their money in the bank because they think it is "safe" are not thinking about the long-term. They are actually losing money. Inflation is eating away at the value of their savings.

Inflation is historically about 3%. If we earn 3% or less on our money, we are losing purchasing power. This means that it costs $0.46 to mail a first class letter instead of 6 cents as it did in 1970. Sending a letter went up at about 5% a year. In order to have enough money to mail a letter in retirement, we are going to need to invest our LONG-TERM money in an investment earning more than 5%. This goes for all the money we will need to buy everything we will need in the future.

There are few investments that we can buy that have the same long-term annual returns of stocks of growing companies. The graph below presents the relative growth of different types of investments and inflation. Over long-periods of time, government bonds grow at a rate a little above the rate of inflation. Large company stocks like GE and P&G grow at a higher rate and thus accumulate larger values in our account. Smaller companies grow much faster and make our account even larger over time. However, as the graph shows, the index line can be very jagged on a monthly and even yearly basis. Values do go up over time.

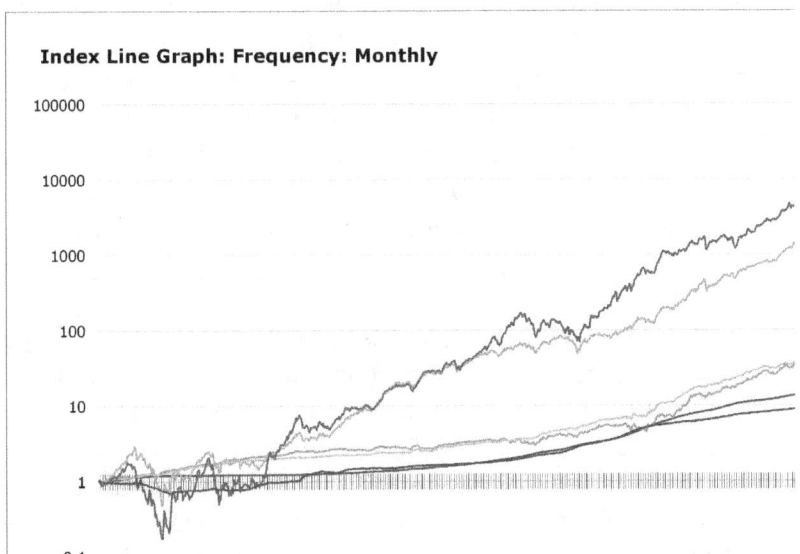

Index Line Graph: Frequency: Monthly

Top line—Small Cap Stocks
2nd line—Large Cap Stocks (S&P 500)
3rd line—US Long-term Corporate Bonds
4th line—Intermediate-term Government Bonds
5th line—US 30 day Government T-bills
6th line—US inflation

Courtesy: Dr. Campbell R. Harvey http://www.duke.edu/~charvey/

This graph makes it pretty clear that in order to accumulate $1,000,000 from monthly contributions, we must buy and hold the securities of growing companies worldwide AND pay **zero** tax on the growth to maximize compounding. We can see clearly that investing in growing company stocks is more likely to get us to our goal in our lifetime than investing in government bonds or a bank savings account.

ThIs graph shows the accumulation over time without paying taxes each year on our earnings or annual fees to an advisor or broker. It does show that over most periods greater than 10 years, our account value grows more with stocks.

Some wealthy people also invest in gold, real estate, and alternative investment schemes. But these investments do NOT usually represent a large portion of their portfolio. These investments do not come without significant costs and significant risk. They do NOT show the same consistent long-term growth pattern that global growing companies do.

According to a number of studies, gold, real estate and other investments have annual average returns under 10%. When we subtract the costs of buying, maintaining and securing these investments, we give up a lot of the gains. We can use an online compounding calculator to become familiar with total accumulations at different rates of return—3, 5, 7, 9, 11, etc. http://www.moneychimp.com/calculator/compound_interest_calcul ator.htm

For instance, if an investment requires taxes to be paid each year, this cancels some of the compounding effect on the total accumulation over time. Since we wish to reach $1 million as soon as possible, we must use a tax-FREE account to hold our investments. Depending on our tax bracket (taxable income) we may reduce our total accumulation by half because we lose the compounding effect. The chart below gives us an idea of what can happen in 30 years. Most pension accounts are tax-DEFERRED not tax-FREE. Taxes have to be paid sometime.

As you have probably guessed, the wealthy have already figured out how to pay less tax on their wealth. The American tax system taxes earned income at higher rates than investment income. Thus we must pay federal and state income taxes, excise taxes, Social Security and Medicare taxes, perhaps unemployment and disability income taxes as well as sales tax on most goods.

For the wealthy, like Warren Buffett, with $65 billions of assets, most of his income is from his company stock gains and dividends. He admitted, "I pay at a lower overall tax rate than all of my office employees." He pays only 17% **total** tax. Listen and weep: http://www.youtube.com/watch?v=Cu5B-2LoC4s.

Most of us pay 30% or more. Most of us have income which is taxed as earned income and goes straight to the government before we have a chance to pay less tax. Even self-employed people must pay taxes as they go—once a quarter.

Tax-FREE v Taxable

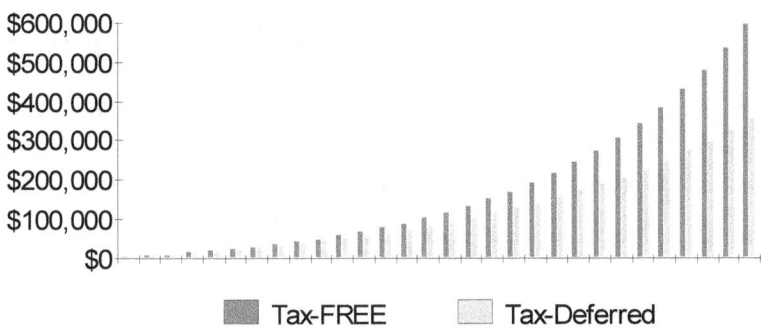

In order for us to become wealthy we must find a way to avoid paying tax on our $1,000,000 account as it accumulates. Traditional pensions, 401k and IRAs just delay taxes—taxes must be paid later as the money comes out of the account AND at higher **earned income** tax rates. Thus even when our investment money is growing it is converted to earned income money for tax purposes. Unlike the wealthy, we would NEVER get to pay their rate of 15% without a tax-FREE low-cost account.

Luckily, there is now a solution for us to match the tax advantage of the wealthy. In fact, only we can use it. Warren Buffett, John Kerry and Mitt Romney earn too much to use this low-cost account.

We use a tax-FREE low-cost account to compound the high returns of the stocks of growing companies over time. We avoid the greatest killer of wealth—taxes—and let time transform our $99,000 ($3,000 X 33) in contributions into $1,000,000. Patience and steady investing make our strategy beat the industry myth of genius stock-pickers.

Compounding high earnings in a low-cost tax-FREE account is how wealth is created.

Various investment accumulations over time

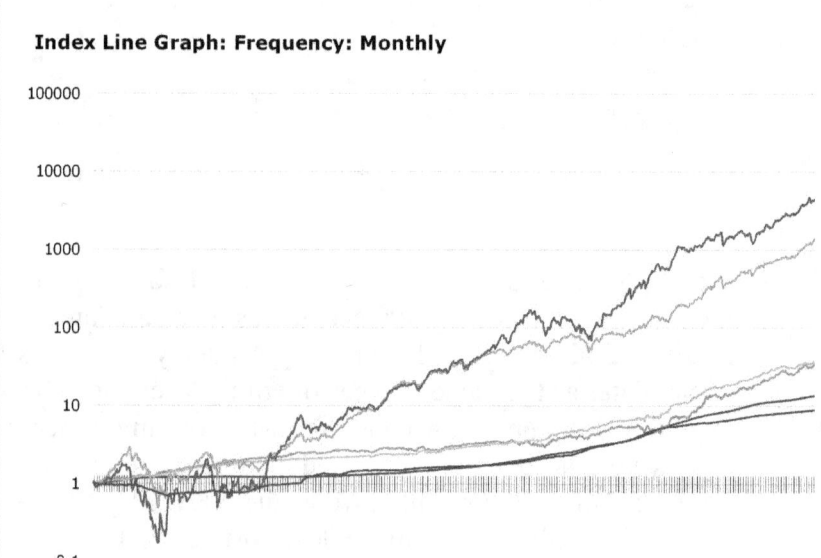

Index Line Graph: Frequency: Monthly

Top line—Small Cap Stocks
2nd line—Large Cap Stocks (S&P 500)
3rd line—US Long-term Corporate Bonds
4th line—Intermediate-term Government Bonds
5th line—US 30 day Government T-bills
6th line—US inflation

Courtesy: Dr. Campbell R. Harvey http://www.duke.edu/~charvey/

2

One low-cost tax-FREE account

The solution to our problem came in 1997. Senator Roth introduced the Roth IRA. This tax-FREE account we call a **Wealth Reserve**™ provides the protection we need to allow our contributions to compound without taxation every year AND later when we take them out, we never have to pay taxes on the earnings, dividends and interest we earn on our money. We even pay less than the tax-advantaged rate of the wealthy!

Ben Franklin was wrong! Only death is certain, not taxes. The only thing we give up with this account is an immediate tax deduction. However, compare the value of paying a little more tax (10%-25% on $3,000) now with paying ZERO tax later. We can spend $30,000 tax-FREE for every $3,000 a year we contributed over time ($1 million/33). We can see the fantastic advantage we now have. This is a better deal than most wealthy people have.

Tax-FREE accumulation and tax-FREE income after age 59.5 is a huge bonus. It is like receiving $300,000 FREE on our $1 million account. Also, because we already paid tax on the contributions, we pay no tax when we take this money out during our lifetimes. This can make a big impact on our borrowing costs when we take money out to buy an appliance, a car, a down payment or living expenses.

Using this account, our total contributions of $99,000 over time grow to over $1,000,000 and we don't have to pay any federal or state income tax on the earnings. WOW! Since we pay no tax, Uncle Sam is really helping us out in meeting our goal. All we have to do is use this special IRS tax haven and keep making contributions.

This low-cost account is the IRS §408 trust we call our **"Wealth Reserve**™**"**. We have to follow the rules to gain this amazing tax advantage but the Roth IRA rules are pretty simple— taxed money goes in and tax-FREE earnings come out after age 59

½. We can take our contributions out anytime.

Why is this account special? Every other type of investment account requires that taxes be paid now or later. Mutual funds declare gains each year just like a bank CD and we need to pay tax. Our retirement accounts and annuities are tax-deferred. We pay tax when we take money out. Even life insurance with cash value requires taxes to be paid unless it is a death benefit to heirs. Even assets like individual stocks or ETFs or our own company equity held for long term gains will require taxes eventually when sold. The gains in a **Wealth Reserve**™ are FREE—no tax ever.

Contributions are limited to $5,500 (2015), but may rise in future years. http://www.irs.gov/publications/p590a There are income limits but most people don't hit the earnings limit of $131,000 (2015) until later. If we are married, the limit is $193,000 (2015). We make our deposit to our **Wealth Reserve**™ automatic so we can't forget to do it each month.

We may also invest in our employer's Roth 401k if it is offered. The contributions grow tax FREE forever. We can contribute up to $18,000 (2015). We will have tax-FREE income from the account later.

We can make contributions to our Roth 401k only if our employer offers it in the retirement plan. Many young people prefer to be taxed at the beginning of their careers since their salaries do not draw high tax rates yet. The contribution limit may be raised in the future.

There are no limits on an employee's income in determining if he or she can make designated Roth 401(k) contributions. If we decide to invest $10,000 a year for 33 years in a low-cost (0.05%) stock fund inside our employer's Roth 401k plan, we could accumulate $2 million with NO income taxation to pay on the earnings. The tax savings might be worth an extra 30% since our federal and state tax payments are avoided.

The catch: If we take the *earnings* out before age 59.5, we must pay income tax, unless we use $10,000 for our first home, are disabled, or die. The account must be open at least 5 years to take money out. However, if we take out *contributions*, we pay no tax. If we pay our 'loan' back to our own account, we can still reach our goal. The hard part is leaving our money alone to grow tax-FREE.

Let's say we need $10,000 to buy a new used car. As we can see from the chart on page 24, taking $10,000 from an account worth $250,000 is very different from taking $10,000 from one worth only $25,000. Both are contributions and are not taxable but borrowing 40% of the account this early stunts its growth.

Our working millionaire would find a way to save the $10,000 separately or keep driving the old car. The power of compounding is too valuable to lose by raiding the account too early. One story about billionaire Buffett will illustrate the habits of the wealthy. Mr Buffett is said to have driven (no chauffeur) his VW Beetle long after he became a multimillionaire. Buffett did not like to lose money and a new car loses 40% of its value quickly. He thought that the $35,000 a new car cost, invested at 12%, is worth triple in about 10 years. So he kept driving the old VW.

Monthly	Accumulation at 12% per year									
	5	10	15	20	25	30	35	40	45	50
$100	$8,167	$23,004	$49,958	$98,925	$187,884	$349,496	$643,095	$1,176,477	$2,145,469	$3,905,834
$200	$16,334	$46,008	$99,916	$197,850	$375,768	$698,992	$1,286,190	$2,352,954	$4,290,938	$7,811,668
$300	$24,501	$69,012	$149,874	$296,775	$563,652	$1,048,488	$1,929,285	$3,529,431	$6,436,408	$11,717,502
$500	$40,835	$115,020	$249,790	$494,625	$939,420	$1,747,480	$3,215,475	$5,882,385	$10,727,346	$19,529,169

Most clients are not that fanatical. They use their contributions to buy a used car to avoid new car depreciation and new appliances, vacations, and other necessities AFTER they have a sizable account. When both family wage earners contribute to their Roth IRAs, they can easily reach a quarter of a million dollars in 15 years. That means $90,000 are contributions and then some of it can be used to pay cash instead of buying on credit.

Wealthy people use their wealth to pay cash because then they never PAY interest. Paying interest on a debt is the reverse of compounding. Someone else is becoming wealthy from us. The wealthy always EARN interest. They use the chart above or the http://www.moneychimp.com/calculator/compound_interest_calcul ator.htm to determine what the real cost of buying something on credit will be just like Buffett did. Why give up $100,000 when we can drive the old car a little longer. Buffett could have bought 100 new cars and it wouldn't have changed his wealth or lifestyle, but he didn't. His habit is to live frugally and not look wealthy.

We can use this account (its contributions) to cover our liability insurance deductibles also. We can save thousands of dollars by using the highest deductibles on our car, home and health insurance. Self-insurance is also the way to avoid any changes in our policy costs. Insurers are less likely to drop us if we don't make claims for small amounts. If we take care of our out-of-pocket medical expenses, we may find a low-cost comprehensive policy if we need to buy health coverage.

The rules for the use of our "**Wealth Reserve**™" account are manageable by ourselves. We don't need an advisor. They are found at irs.gov/retirement/article/0,,id=137307,00.html. Our account trustee can answer most questions. We don't need to pay an attorney. All of the large low-cost mutual funds firms are trustees. We will discuss the best firms available below.

We can start this account with any of the firms with no upfront charges. Most do charge an annual fee for the investments and bookkeeping. We will consider the specific investment options later. We will use low-cost firms with fees under 0.2%.

It is important to pick a trustee with the least costs since over time the annual costs can really destroy our accumulations. For instance, if we use a brokerage firm as trustee, we might have to pay 2-3% each year on the balance. The difference is huge. If both spouses have a low-cost account with contributions of $250 a month for 33 years, they could accumulate $2,000,000. If they use a high-cost broker/advisor, *both* accounts may hit only $400,000. Depending on earnings of 3.79% using a broker/advisor, they could really hurt themselves. We need to avoid the costs. We will compare firms below.

We can open our account at any age as long as we have *earned* income. Any job will do. We don't even need a job requiring a W-2 to prove it. A part-time, weekend or night job will do. Any cash-only work will also qualify. Accountants recommend that receipts and records be maintained. We could even work for ourselves in a home-office business.

Nontaxable distributions from a Roth IRA won't affect our eligibility for student aid either. Later, in retirement, this money won't affect our social security benefits as of the rules today.

We can make contributions to both our individual Roth IRA and our Roth account at work (401k, 403b, 457b). The limits change each year, so check Pub 590a: https://www.irs.gov/pub/irs-pdf/p590a.pdf. The 2015 limits are $5,500 and $18,000. (If we are age 50 or older, we can make an extra "catch-up" contribution to both ($1,000) and ($5,500).)

Avoiding taxes and fees on our annual gains supercharges

our accumulations. This special account is the IRS §408 trust we call a "**Wealth Reserve**™". We have to follow the rules of a Roth IRA to gain this amazing tax advantage. The rules are pretty simple: pay smaller tax on contributions now in exchange for NO tax on huge gains later. We can use the contributions to avoid paying interest to banks for our major purchases. We earn interest, we don't pay interest. The **Wealth Reserve**™ is the perfect tax shelter for working people. And it is free to set up and costs little to run each year. In the future, we can spend $30,000 tax-FREE on every $3,000 we invest today.

That is the *miracle of compounding in a low-cost account.*

Client Tom's account, investing $3,000 per year, 1962-2003

24%	3,720
16%	7,795
12%	12,091
-10%	13,582
24%	20,561
11%	26,153
-8%	26,821
4%	31,013
14%	38,775
19%	49,713
-14%	45,333
-26%	35,766
37%	53,110
24%	69,576
-8%	66,770
6%	73,956
18%	90,809
32%	123,827
-5%	120,486
22%	150,653
21%	185,920
6%	200,255
32%	268,297
19%	322,843
5%	342,135
17%	403,808
32%	536,987
-3%	523,787
31%	690,091
8%	748,538
10%	826,692
2%	846,286
38%	1,172,015
23%	1,445,268
33%	1,926,197
28%	2,469,372
21%	2,991,570
-9%	2,725,059
-12%	2,403,420
-22%	1,874,601
29%	2,412,905

3

Compound high earnings

Compounding the earnings is key. The rich get richer—the top 1% take 23.5% of all income (up from 8.9%). And, as many millionaires have said, "the first million is the hardest." If we start with $3,000, it will take us about 33 years of investing $3,000 a year in stock funds to reach $1,000,000. (And only in a low-cost tax-FREE account.) However, when we reach a million dollars, we only have to double our money to reach $2 million. Investors in stock funds, earning 10-12% on average, do this in about 9 years without adding new money. Our tax-FREE account makes it easier to reach our goal. Compounding makes it happen.

Compounding of high earnings means that we make money on our last period's accumulations. The progression looks like the client's account values on the previous page. Notice that our balance can double in a couple of good years. This happens because we are not just adding $3,000 per year, but adding up to 38% of the previous year's accumulation to our balance. We are making money on top of our money with no extra effort on our part. During this 40 year period, this client lost money some years. In fact, they lost 14% and then 26% back to back, but then made 37% and 24%. He retired with $2.4 million and growing.

Wealthy people don't panic. They have learned that compounding over the long-term is the only way they can build wealth. Only the promoter gets rich in get-rich-quick schemes. To reach our goal, we know there will be setbacks. No business grows steadily upward all the time. The rich have seen the losses before and they don't sell their assets in a panic.

We will buy assets that "grow by themselves." We will have security because our **_purchasing power_** will grow over time. If we doubt that the wealthy invest in the stock market for security, take a look at the long-term returns for various Vanguard mutual funds where they put their money. These funds have provided investors with $1,000,000 or more for their retirement. During the 2007-8 recession, Vanguard had inflows not outflows.

The wealthy earn 10% to 12% on their money. We could buy all ten Vanguard funds and receive 10-12% total return with less risk than owning just one. When one fund is down, others are up.

2015 Total Return	Fund	Long-term Return	Longevity
1.4%	500 Index	10.8%*	since 1976
-21.5%	Energy	10.3%	since 1984
-3.3%	Extended Market Idx	10.6%	since 1987
12.7%	Health	17.3%	since 1984
-0.7%	International Growth	10.3%	since 1981
2.6%	PRIMECAP	13.5%	since 1984
-3.6%	Small Cap Index	10.5%	since 1960
1.3%	Wellesley Income	9.9%	since 1970
-3.3%	Windsor	11.3%	since 1958
-3.2%	Windsor II	10.6%	since 1985
-1.7%	Average	11.5%	

*Average Annual Returns as of 12/31/15.

This kind of security comes from our regular contributions … and patience. The miracle of compounding works its magic on our **Wealth Reserve**™ when we give it TIME. The wealthy give their money <u>time to compound</u>. They don't take it out and they try not to pay tax every year on the gains. They maintain their contribution schedule because each $3,000 is worth $30,000 to them later. They use the compound interest calculator so they know the future value: <u>moneychimp.com/calculator/compound_interest_calculator.htm</u>.

Compounding of high earnings requires patience but has a big bang. Most people who become wealthy have to put up with years of slow growth in their account. At the beginning of the accumulation, especially if we have a loss or two, we are very tempted to get discouraged and quit making contributions. The account just doesn't seem to adding up to an inspiring total.

It took this client 21 years to get to $150,000. Then it only took 14 years to get to a $1,172,015. After only 4 years, it became $3,000,000. Shortly thereafter he "lost" over a million dollars!

This client stuck with it and was successful in reaching the goal but there are many who did not. Most people who are not wealthy already, have a hard time believing it can happen with their patience. They just don't have the experience of how compounding works to keep faith in its outcome eventually.

If you already have a **Wealth Reserve**™ with significant values, you can use it to do your gift and estate planning. You don't have to take the money out beginning at age 70½ like the regular IRA or pension. You can let it grow. You can name your family members as beneficiaries which will be effective for both property law and income tax purposes. Obviously, as beneficiary, your grandchild could just liquidate the account and thus lose the value for their "Gift of a Lifetime." Wealthy people use a knowledgable attorney to make sure their wealth passes to those who make the most of it.

Once an account becomes sizable, we don't need to add contributions to it. Usually, by the time we stop regular employment, we aren't making contributions. This account cannot accept contributions unless they are the result of earned income. Some wealthy people continue to work after age 65 because they love what they do and want to continue. Obviously, they don't need to work. The miracle of compounding continues.

One of the best examples of the potential of growth by compounding is seen in the accumulation of investor Anne Scheiber. With below average wages, this woman invested in quality companies which paid dividends and gains. She reinvested her dividends and gains and at her death gave $22 million to Yeshiva University for a scholarship designed to help support deserving women.

Getting "the first million is the hardest." Since we don't make millions, compounding high earnings is the only way we are going to reach our goal in our lifetime. Compounding works because we leverage TIME in our favor in a low-cost tax-FREE account.

As Warren Buffett said,

"My wealth has come from a combination of living in America, some lucky genes, and **compound interest**."

The annual returns of growing companies

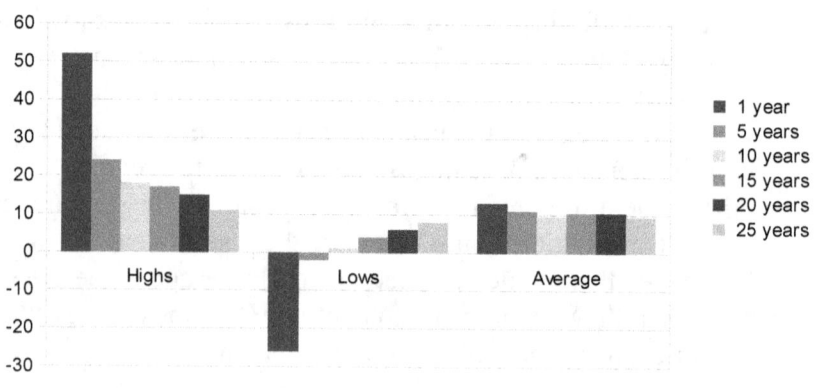

Range of annual returns of stocks, 1950 – 2000

4

Automate contributions

One of the techniques for building wealth is to maintain consistent contributions to our **Wealth Reserve**™. This helps take our emotions out of the process of building wealth. If we do not watch the stock market or our account balance regularly, we will be less likely to panic. If we don't have to write and send the contribution each month, we don't think about how our account is doing.

Our normal reaction to having money in an account is to watch it, guard it, think about how it is doing, compare its size and rate of growth. All of these actions are fine for a broker account. But as a silent partner in growing companies, this is not wise. We have to believe that global businesses will continue to grow. However, most people don't look at their wealth building in that way. Most people do not think of this account as a stake in many growing businesses.

One way we can help change our thinking is to try to put the account out of our immediate concern by making the contributions automatic. Like the Social Security contributions we make every payday, the contributions come out of our pay automatically. This can happen easily with a Roth 401k since our Plan administrator will deduct the amount we specify at Plan enrollment. In the same manner, we can have the Roth IRA trustee debit our checking account automatically every period.

As one client told me, "I never see the deduction, so I never miss it." Of course this client has already identified the $250 he has committed to his $1,000,000 future. He says that he would just waste the $250 anyway. He had been doing that for years because he never took the trouble to set his goals for short-term and long-term timelines. He took my advice and went through his spending on financial services. He used our Guides to find the $250 a month he was wasting on products and services he would never use or need. In Dan Keppel's Guides, amazon.com/Insiders-Guides-Discount-Financial-Services/, you will find "tricks of the trade" that we insiders use to buy directly from quality manufacturers.

Many people have trouble keeping up the habit of investing every month. Some emergency always interupts this process. The delay in the periodic contributions causes the compounding effect to be reduced. The interruption is like starting the investment process late. This chart shows us what starting early or not putting off the investments can do. Over time, the delay compounds the lack of accumulation. Starting 5 years later means ending up with HALF the amount we were shooting for. It is hard to believe that missing that $250 a month for 5 years or $15,000 can reduce our total from $600,000 to $300,000. It's easy to say **I will start later**.

The Value of Starting Early

This is why our contributions to the account should not pass through our hands. We should have the money taken directly from our bank account by the trustee. Contributions are after-tax so you can take them, if necessary, with no tax payable. Nontaxable distributions from a Roth IRA won't affect your eligibility for student aid either. Later, in retirement, this money won't affect your Social Security benefits as of the rules today.

The second reason why this technique for developing wealth works is that when contributions are automatic, we do not have the temptation to try to time the market. Many people want to know the secret to timing the market so that they can invest right at the bottom of market cycles and sell at the peak of the market.

Unfortunately, it is a myth that anyone can do this at all. Again, this is a misconception of how building wealth works. Yes there are lucky gamblers. However, luck lasts a short time. We want our wealth to be permanent. We want over $1,000,000 tax-FREE. We are silent partners in building businesses that produce dividends and gains over time. We are not placing our contributions on red or black at the casino.

Our account grows with steady contributions because in the month we buy $250 of company stocks in a mutual fund, we receive less shares when the price is high and more shares when the price is low. Studies have shown that this is better than investing our $3,000 all at once. It is not possible to know when the shares we buy will be at their lowest cost in the year going forward. Again, over time, we will own more shares at the least cost because we are buying more when the price is low.

This can be illustrated by considering how hard it is to find the lowest price at any given time in the market. There were ONLY 40 days from 1950 to 2007 that produced 70% of all the S&P 500 index's total returns. That is 40 days out of 14,528. We can't possibly know when to buy into the businesses represented in the mutual fund we are using. We will lose money if we try to time the market. See John Bogle's analysis in *Don't Count on It*, p 169.

The key to building wealth is steady growth. We have seen that over time, stocks of growing companies have the most consistent record of providing 10-12% annual returns. We just don't know which companies and which time to invest are best. Luckily, we don't have to know. We need to understand the bigger picture.

The bigger picture is that we want our low-cost account to grow exponentially. See page 30. We want to take advantage of the miracle of compounding. Since we don't have a million dollars, we are going to have to be patient to acquire it. We want every dollar we invest to count. We have $250 a month to invest so we have to rely on consistent buying of shares to reach our goal.

Accumulations double in value every 8-10 years if they are concentrated in the top two lines. Of course the stock market doesn't move up at 10-12% EACH year. However, our low-cost account will double and double and double so that by age 65, we could have over $1 million. Notice how the account values in the chart on page 24 for our client move to $1 million in 35 years, even with 3 years of losses. Of course, a million dollars will be worth less in the future because of inflation. But we will certainly appreciate our account values later at 11% not 3.79%.

Cumulative Wealth

Index Line Graph: Frequency: Monthly

Top line—Small Cap Stocks
2nd line—Large Cap Stocks (S&P 500)
3rd line—US Long-term Corporate Bonds
4th line—Intermediate-term Government Bonds
5th line—US 30 day Government T-bills
6th line—US inflation

Courtesy: Dr. Campbell R. Harvey http://www.duke.edu/~charvey/

And the bonus of this geometric account growth is that it does not quit even after we stop adding our monthly contributions. Once the account has reached a certain mass, let's say after 30 years of contributions or $90,000, it will keep compounding. On page 34 we show you how this worked for contributions of $2,000 to a virtual account invested in the U.S. stock market (500 Index fund) over time.

We can see in the chart "Cumulative Wealth" above that over time, wealth accumulates at different rates depending on the type of assets we buy. For anyone who invested in smaller companies over any given 15 year period, the benefits were outstanding. For each $1,000 invested in 1940, $3,000,000 was the total return by the 1990's. Investing more cautiously in the large companies of the

S&P 500, for instance, our $1,000 would have grown to almost a $1,000,00 by 2000. Yes, the lines are not perfectly straight, but growing $250 a month to $1,000,000 is definitely worth the ups and downs. Inflation is designated by the bottom line here. Putting all our money in a managed account would accumulate at a rate represented by the 5th line near the bottom.

Of course, these different rates of wealth accumulation assume two important factors—NO taxes and LOW costs. We have eliminated the first killer of wealth—TAXES—by using a tax-FREE account. Costs of the investment type we use can also kill our total accumulations. My whole industry is built on the extraction of these costs from the accounts of investors. We must use low-cost stock funds without selling to reach our goal.

One of the most difficult parts of building wealth is sticking with the program. If we put our monthly contributions on automatic, we will have no interruptions. If we instruct our trustee to debit our savings or checking account every month, we have a high probability of meeting our goals over time. We forget we are investing in our future and thus we actually create one.

This is how *our low-cost tax-FREE account* works. We make contributions, pay no tax, pay low costs and compounding drives wealth higher than a broker can.

Wall Street firms and their salepeople earn money from our money.
**We put up the money and take all the risks and
they collect 1-3%** per year.
Sweet!

Year	Returns	Balance $2,000	Balance	Balance	Balance
1950	31%	$2,620			
1951	24%	$5,729			
1952	18%	$9,120			
1953	-1%	$11,009			
1954	52%	$19,773			
1955	31%	$28,523			
1956	5%	$32,049			
1957	-11%	$30,304			
1958	43%	$46,194			
1959	12%	$53,978			
1960	1%	$56,538			
1961	26%	$73,757			
1962	-8%	$69,697			
1963	24%	$88,904			
1964	16%	$105,449			
1965	12%	$120,342			
1966	-10%	$110,108			
1967	24%	$139,014			
1968	11%	$156,526			
1969	-8%	$145,844	2,000		
1970	4%	$153,757	2,080		
1971	14%	$177,563	4,651		
1972	19%	$213,681	7,915		
1973	-14%	$185,485	8,527		
1974	-26%	$138,739	7,790		
1975	37%	$192,813	13,412		
1976	24%	$241,568	19,111		
1977	-8%	$224,082	19,422		
1978	6%	$239,647	22,707		
1979	18%	$285,144	29,155	2,000	
1980	32%	$379,030	41,124	2,640	
1981	-5%	$361,978	40,968	4,408	
1982	22%	$444,053	52,421	7,818	
1983	21%	$539,724	65,850	11,879	
1984	6%	$574,228	71,921	14,712	
1985	32%	$760,621	97,575	22,060	
1986	19%	$907,519	118,494	28,632	
1987	5%	$954,995	126,519	32,163	
1988	17%	$1,119,684	150,367	39,971	
1989	32%	$1,480,623	201,125	55,402	2,000
1990	-3%	$1,438,144	197,031	55,680	1,940
1991	31%	$1,886,589	260,731	75,560	5,161
1992	8%	$2,039,676	283,749	83,765	7,734
1993	10%	$2,245,843	314,324	94,342	10,708
1994	2%	$2,292,800	322,651	98,268	12,962
1995	38%	$3,166,824	448,018	138,370	20,647
1996	23%	$3,897,654	553,522	172,656	27,856
1997	33%	$5,186,540	738,844	232,292	39,709
1998	28%	$6,641,331	948,281	299,894	53,387
1999	21%	$8,038,430	1,149,839	365,291	67,019
2000	-9%	$7,316,791	1,048,174	334,235	62,807
2001	-12%	$6,447,855	925,203	296,223	57,095
2002	-22%	$5,024,437	722,291	232,316	46,035
2003	29%	$6,459,474	930,787	301,119	61,730
2004	11%	$7,164,483	1,034,274	336,099	70,664
2005	5%	$7,512,677	1,084,540	352,433	74,098
2006	15%	$8,694,884	1,259,259	412,409	90,450
2007	5%	$9,163,538	1,327,133	434,638	95,325
2008	-39%	$5,601,431	813,388	268,074	60,754
2009	27%	$7,116,358	952,155	342,993	79,699
2010	15%	$8,186,112	1,097,278	396,742	93,954
2011	2%	$8,347,378	1,118,894	404,558	95,805
2012	16%	$9,666,264	1,295,679	468,478	110,942
2013	32%	$12,759,468	1,710,296	618,390	146,443
Avg.	12%	12%	11%	13%	11%

Ibbotson Associates **Stocks average 11.4% per year, bonds 5%, CDs 3%.** Stocks have gone up as much as 54% and as low as –43% in 1 year, up to 28% or down to –12% in 5 years, up 20% or down 0% in 10 years, up 18% or up 3% in 20 years. Short term bonds have gone up 14% or up 0% in 1 year, up 11% or up 0% in 5 years, up 9% or up 0% in 10 years, up 10% or up 1% in 20 years.

5

Low-cost mutual funds

**"In every single time period and data point tested,
low-cost funds beat high-cost funds."**

According to an unbiased <u>Morningstar</u> study, low-cost funds beat
high-cost funds PERIOD. The myth of Wall Street is that you *must*
pay more for good performance. Not true. We all know that in
most groceries' prices, paying more (for packaging and TV
commercials) does not guarantee the best product.

The **best predictor** of your investing and wealth building
success is *low cost*. It is common sense that there are just too many
variables in the success of growing companies' stocks for anyone
to be able to pick them in advance on a consistent basis. A low-cost
stock mutual fund provides the best chance of maximizing our
accumulations as the market leaders change over time.

Contrary to Wall Street's hype, it does not matter which
stocks are rising or falling at any given time. If our account holds a
broad representation of stocks and our investment costs are low,
we will benefit over the long haul. We own them all at cost!

Since the annual returns of stock funds have averaged 10-
12% over time, we want to pick the lowest cost mutual fund
available. A stock fund that reflects the overall market is called an
index fund. This kind of fund, explained below, costs only 0.05%
(<u>$5 per $10,000</u>). Our account will compound at or near the 10-
12% over time since the costs are low compared to ones that
charge <u>1.5-3%</u>. If we trade high-cost stocks and funds in our
account, we will earn 3.79% over time. These funds pay managers
high salaries with expensive bonuses. The fund owners and sales
staff are paid well also. This is the cash cow of Wall Street.

The chart below makes it clear. Over time, the costs we pay
each year will cut our total accumulation by a HALF or more.
Instead of compounding at 10-12% annually on average, some

people give up 1.5-3% of the earnings on their money to the middle person. They end up with less.

Cost Matters: 0.19% v 1.68%

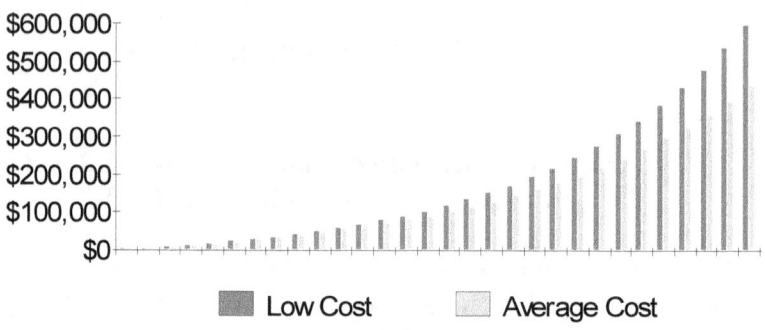

Wall Street says that we can earn more by paying a star manager to pick the right stocks on an ongoing basis. The money "experts" say we get what we pay for and a proven stock-picking manager will overcome the extra costs and make more for us.

The problem is that this myth has been proven wrong. The lowest cost funds don't pay a star manager and owner big bucks but come out ahead over time. There are simply too many variables for anyone or computer program to pick the winning stocks all the time in advance. Some of the lowest cost funds are called index funds. When we buy an index, we are buying a piece of many companies that reflect the market. This gives us the same annual returns as the overall market over time. We pay tiny expenses.

Many studies have proven that index funds beat funds run by stock pickers most of the time. Low-cost index funds beat 86% of funds with a stock-picking manager. *BusinessWeek* Apr 2009. http://www.businessweek.com/investing/insights/blog/archives/2009/04/where_have_all.html.

When we investigate the experiences of the best money managers in the world, we find they recommend index funds to most people who invest as silent partners in real businesses. Here are their statements:

Warren Buffett is probably history's greatest investor, in terms of results with $60 BILLION ($60 thousand million dollars) so far. He buys *companies* that provide valuable services to a great

number of people. His company owns parts of Coke, GEICO Fruit of Loom, Benjamin Moore, Acme Bricks, etc berkshirehathaway.com/
Buffett told Reuters:

"A very low-cost index is going to beat a majority of the amateur-managed money or professionally-managed money."

Compare the odds of selecting the correct mutual fund. A fund's chance of beating the market in EACH year is 3 out of 100. nytimes.com/2009/02/22/your-money/stocks-and-bonds/22stra.html

Peter Lynch, brilliant manager, Magellan Fund "…you'd be just as well off if you'd invested in the S&P 500." *One Up on Wall Street*, 1989, p. 240.

Jonathan Clements, formerly ***The Wall Street Journal***
"Most people can do it themselves. ... By indexing, you don't just ensure that you will do better than most other investors. You will also enjoy the advantage of 'relative certainty.' . . . For most investors, Vanguard will be the place to go." *You've Lost It, Now What? How to beat the bear market and still retire on time*, 2003, p. 62, 70.

Charles D. Ellis, money managers' consultant
"The premise . . . that professional investment managers *can* beat the market . . . appears to be false. It is a loser's game. … clients would have done better in a market fund." Returns are "splendidly predictable—on average and over time." *Investment Policy, How to Win the Loser's Game*, 1985, p. 5, 20, 34.

Jane Bryant Quinn, consumer advisor
"I'm a longtime booster of index mutual funds. These funds follow the market as a whole. Tons of research has shown that most money managers don't beat the markets they invest in, after costs. Maybe your own stocks or funds have excelled in the past couple of years. But in most cases, you've also been taking extra risk. The odds of superior performance are against you, in the long run. Indexing puts the odds on your side." *Los Angeles BJ*, May 8, 2000

Charles Schwab founder, discount broker
"I put my money where my mouth is: most of the mutual fund investments I have are in index funds, approximately 75%. My core investments are index funds. Experienced investors have discovered that in any given year, on average, only 20 to 30 percent of mutual funds outperform the market. That is why I recommend index funds…"
Mr. Schwab tells of one of his friends who owned many well-run funds. After keeping track of all the dividends, taxes, reinvestments tax basis and statements, he found he earned the same return as the index of these funds. After selling them all, he bought the index fund. He has "what he wanted in the first place: diversification, tax advantages, one statement, and lower expenses." *Guide to Financial Independence*, 1998, pp. 90, 103, 111.

Motley Fool, Internet site about investing
"Almost **everything** that you will ever read about mutual funds beyond, "Buy an index fund." is superfluous to your long-term success in investing in mutual funds." Fool.com.

Walter Updegrave, senior editor, *Money*
"Mutual fund picking would be easier if there was one you could count on to outperform 70% or so of its competitors over long stretches of a decade or more. It's called an index fund. Although less than 10% of investors own an index fund, they are "one of the best-kept secrets" on Wall Street. My unabashed aim is to convince you to put at least a part of your money into one or more of these funds. You have a far less than a 50% chance of beating the market…. I strongly recommend that you make index funds your primary holding…." *The Right Way to Invest in Mutual Funds*, 1996, p 189-194.

Andrew Tobias, financial writer
"Scrimp and save, putting whatever you can into no-load, low-expense stock market index funds, both U.S. and foreign. You will do better than 80% of your friends and neighbors." *My Vast Fortune*, 1997, p. 158.

There are many books written on the subject of index and

"managed" funds. If you wish to vanquish the hype and understand investing, skim *A Random Walk Down Wall Street* by Princeton University's Burton Malkiel. Here are the reasons why smart insiders use low-cost funds:

1. Both stock and bond index funds provide better returns than 86% of managed funds for periods greater than 10 years.
2. You earn more because you pay lower costs and taxes.
3. Low-cost funds build greater wealth over time.
4. Low-cost funds can be less volatile because they reflect whole sectors of the market.
5. Low-cost funds offer better diversification.
6. You know what you are paying for. No high-salary managers.
7. Low-cost funds don't require you to hope the manager will predict the future correctly. The odds of doing it are 1 in 15,000 each year separately. Over time, all funds provide average returns minus their costs.
8. Low-cost funds are easy to buy.

> "Professional money management is a gigantic rip-off."
> Bill Gross, star bond manager, *Everything You've Heard About Investing is Wrong*

Summary of many studies about index investing

First, fund managers try to predict the future of the market when they buy and sell securities in their funds. There is no proof this can be done well over time. Yesterday's winners are usually tomorrow's losers. The AVERAGE market return has been 10-12%, so a few managers will beat the average by luck—Just not the same ones every year. nytimes.com/2008/07/13/business/13stra.html **Second**, the costs of the manager, their staff and operations must be paid for by you whether or not they earn you a dime. It is always better to pay as little as possible for the same performance. Costs can take 33% of your returns over time. Surprisingly, while the stock index rose 11.11%, investors with high paid managers averaged only **3.79%** annually over the last 30 years (QAIB). DALBARinc.
Third, high cost managers get paid for increasing the size of their

funds, not for making you rich. Bringing in more money is a full-time job. It is expensive to market the funds given that there are now thousands available. It is inevitable that popular funds will grow until they produce average returns with high expenses. Managers want to be rich, not right.

Fourth, there is much less chance of you being treated poorly by fund management if the structure and governance are customer-oriented like Vanguard's and TIAA-CREF's are.

Fifth, many professional managers and Wall Street insiders place their core assets in low-cost index funds.

Sixth, Warren Buffett recommends Vanguard index funds for his own family. http://www.amazon.com/Warren-Buffetts-Vanguard-Funds-Retirement/dp/1496148592

The best predictor of the success in investing is cost. Usually the least expensive funds that match market averages beat the more expensive managed funds over time. Low-cost market index funds buy all the securities represented in a broad market. The goal of an index fund is to match its market. Low-cost index funds have provided returns that beat 80-90% of managed funds over the long-term. No manager has been able to predict the future so the returns regress to the mean—averaging 10-12%.

The smart money is on the averages not the long shot.

"In every single time period and data point tested, low-cost funds beat high-cost funds."

6

Global growth

If we want to have at least a $1,000,000 tax-FREE, we need a way to make it happen—a strategy. To have a nest egg of $1 million requires that we know how and where to invest, invest regularly, invest properly, monitor accumulations along the way, and get help when we need it. We need a clear plan that takes only one hour to set up and only one hour per year to manage. Complicated plans just don't work for most people. Complicated strategies cost more than they are worth for most people.

Picking *individual* stocks as a strategy is not likely to work for us. Professional managers and day traders have had limited success **over time**. Our strategy is to build wealth as a silent partner in growing global companies. Since it is unlikely that we (or anyone else) will be able to pick the next Google or Apple, we invest in a large group of firms. We do not need to fear picking the wrong one or picking one at the wrong time. As the founder of the largest mutual fund firm, John Bogle, says: "Don't look for the needle. Buy the haystack."

This is contrary to the myth of Wall Street 'professionals.' They make their living claiming to find the needle every year and we pay the price. Professionals promise that they can find the next big one and we pay them well because we want to be rich.

Like the lottery, we kid ourselves into thinking that "someone has to win, why not me." We don't believe we are wasting our money even though our rational mind knows that our chance of winning is low. Managed funds don't beat the market most of the time. The odds are like those of a lottery—18 million to 1. Like the lottery, when we invest in a managed fund to "beat the market" we don't count up the costs of the "tickets." We may buy $25 worth of tickets a week and end up winning $1,000 in a year. We spent $1,200 for $1,000. The odds remain over time.

In the same manner, a mutual fund manager advertises that

their fund has "beaten" the market and so we pay 1.5-3% of our assets every year. Over time we find that while the stock market index rose 11% annually over 30 years, we earned only 3.79%. This is what happened to retail investors according to Dalbar's QAIB recent study. http://www.etfguide.com/why-do-so-many-investors-self-destruct/

Some of us keep switching to the hot investments according to the advertising we see every month. Some are always chasing the last most successful mutual fund. Some buy the winner at the high point because they want the winner. They sell the security when it falls and they want the next high flier. Over time they never earn the return promised in the hype.

In this way, costs can take 63% of our returns over time. Each time we sell and buy, we give up earnings and perhaps part of our money if we use a sales person charging 5%. Even if we stay with one managed account that has annual fees of 1.5-3%, we are killing the miracle of compounding.

Using the compounding calculator, we can see that our accumulation drops to $0.4 million if we earn 3.79% instead of 11% annually. We could have $1 million in 35 years at 10-12%. http://www.moneychimp.com/calculator/compound_interest_calcul ator.htm

Another Wall Street myth is that investing in market index funds will produce mediocre returns. It is true that the returns will be close to the returns of the market. However, historically the market returns are the ones that are somewhat predictable. Investing in growing companies provides no guaranteed return but the average returns have held steady since the 1930s when they started keeping records.

Wall Street history is littered with strategies that were said to beat the market. The brilliant stock pickers have also come and gone. Today, though, which one of the new ones are we going to invest with? No one knows. The ONLY thing we really know is that the averages of broad market indexes have produced 10-12% on average each year.

For example, some of my clients use these Vanguard mutual funds which have earned over 11% for a long time. Of course, there is no guarantee of future returns, but they have all done fairly well. Most started with the 500 Index and added companies in the Energy, Health and International sectors. These

10 funds have done well over time. Many investors pick Vanguard funds because the funds are well run at cost. No "bells and whistles." No expensive managers and overhead. No owner taking profits from our investment returns.

2013 Total Return	Fund	Long-term Return*	Longevity
32.3%	500 Index	11.0%*	since 1976
18.4%	Energy	13.2%	since 1984
38.4%	Extended Market Idx	11.2%	since 1987
43.2%	Health	17.1%	since 1984
23.0%	International Growth	11.2%	since 1981
39.7%	PRIMECAP	13.7%	since 1984
37.6%	Small Cap Index	10.9%	since 1960
9.2%	Wellesley Income	10.1%	since 1970
36.1%	Windsor	11.6%	since 1958
30.7%	Windsor II	11.1%	since 1985
30.9%	Average	12.1%	

*Average Annual Returns as of 12/31/13.

My clients are long-term investors, not speculators. They believe that investments in low-cost funds (index and managed) are their best chance of reaching their goals. They have been rewarded for that belief. Vanguard has many low-cost funds and their service is better than most funds.

Remember, we are investing for the long-term. Most pension funds are invested in stock and bond indexes. Even though the market fell 22% in 2002 and jumped 29% in 2003, the average was still holding. Average returns mean we do not suffer the lowest lows nor the highest highs. They regress to the mean: 10-12%.

Most of the largest growing companies in the world are held by these funds. Large US firms are now earning at least half of their profits overseas so we are benefiting from growth around the world. This is important because we don't want to miss important earnings progress as the developing nations like China and India expand their economies.

We don't know exactly which companies will be winners so we participate in all of them. We want to own some smaller growing companies too. If they become successful, they will move to the large company funds. We are exposed to almost all areas of the global economy by buying shares of these mutual funds at the lowest cost. We suffer the ups and downs of the markets just like every investor. However, we see that some funds do better at certain times while others do worse. Together we see clients hitting their goal of 10-12% average annual returns.

This type of investing has the greatest chance of avoiding severe swings in the balance of our accumulation. This type of strategy—investing in different types and sizes of companies in different sectors around the world—is called Modern Portfolio Theory.

Modern Portfolio Theory

Some clients use the MPT strategy to control risk while increasing returns. MPT (Moneychimp.com/articles/risk/riskintro.htm) holds that if we put our eggs in different baskets of assets that grow at different times, then the value of all our eggs grows with fewer ups and downs. We can manage the ups and downs of equity funds by buying different ones over time. Higher risk assets are small caps, REITs and foreign stocks. This strategy earns 10-12% with 30% less volatility.

Members assemble asset classes (see http://www.callan.com/ research/download/?file=periodic%2ffree%2f757.pdf) that fit their risk-reward tastes. According to this Nobel Prize-winning strategy moneychimp.com/articles/risk/portfolio.htm, a high return asset with a low correlation to other assets in the portfolio can actually reduce the volatility of the whole. It may be possible to earn high returns with less risk **overall** as each asset goes up and down at different times. See the example at fool.com/personal-finance/retirement/2007/03/06/5-steps-to-salvage-your-retirement.aspx.

The past provides only PROBABLE futures. But isn't $1,000,000 (plus or minus $100,000) better than $200,000. Your $250-per-month deposit in a managed account for 33 years will be worth only $200,000 compared with about $1 million from your low-cost tax-FREE account. Every investor would be better off with $1 million than $200,000 from an advisor/broker.

When clients begin investing, they cannot buy all 10 Vanguard funds at once with $250 per month. Vanguard has minimums on all funds so they can keep their expenses low for everyone.

There are two ways to start our **Wealth Reserve**™.

The easiest way is to save $250 a month in our savings account until we have the $1,000 minimum for Vanguard's entry fund: STAR #56. We can open the Roth IRA by phone or online: STAR minimum is $1,000. Most Vanguard funds need $3,000 to start. We can keep contributing to this index fund until we have $3,000 for the 500 Index and then $3,000 for the Extended Market fund, etc. Vanguard is at 800.551.8631.

The second way to begin is to open a Roth IRA at TIAA-CREF, the world's largest pension company, primarily for educational and research institutions. Low expenses and low initial contributions make TIAA-CREF an organization we can stay with for life. TIAA-CREF 800.842.2888.

At TIAA-CREF.org, we can make application and begin immediately with an automatic monthly contribution of $100 or more from our bank account. We can follow how the assets grow by themselves. TIAA-CREF has two funds that provide us with the diversity of companies worldwide: TIAA-CREF Equity Index and TIAA International Equity.

Request a prospectus (owner's manual) for each fund you will be using at Vanguard or TIAA-CREF. Both mutual fund firms have experienced salaried representatives that provide accurate information about accounts and funds. Both offer low-cost index funds that hold a broad representation of the market returns of 10-12%. This is a building block to accumulating wealth.

Both firms are focused on you, not on profits.

This strategy provides long-term growth of 10-12% annually on average with the benefit of avoiding single company or industry failures. It provides exposure to new growth potential around the world with less risk than holding one company, one sector, or one country. This is how our low-cost tax-FREE account grows over time. Pay less, get more.

It is the amount we KEEP that matters!

Cost matters!

10-year returns, all equity funds

Low-cost quartile
High-cost quartile

- Actual return*: 10.2% / 6.8%
- Risk-adjusted return: 10.3% / 6.5%
- After-tax return*: 8.3% / 4.3%

*Source: Morningstar avg. ann. returns for 10 yrs ended 8/03.

7

Expenses less than income

We need to find at least $250 per month to invest in order to build our **Wealth Reserve**™. We can build wealth by following the strategy outlined in the previous chapters, but we need to have at least $250 available in the first place. In my experience, it doesn't matter how much people earn, most say they don't have the $250 a month to invest for their future. "Today is hard enough," they complain.

Yes, that may well be, but if we don't find the $250 we won't have a very happy tomorrow. We have to go back to our goal. We want to build wealth: accumulating $1,000,000 over time. Based on the way wealth compounds, we need to identify at least $250 a month on a permanent basis—35 years. We need to be consistent for the miracle of compounding to work.

Budget is a dirty word so we won't use it. No one wants to be restricted in their spending. Even the people who know they are wasting $100 a month on the lottery, still play. I know it satisfies an immediate riches fantasy. I know because I used to play every week like many others who never saw the power of compounding.

I want to explain how we can find the $250 a month to invest from a different perspective. If we are going to spend all of our income, we need to adopt a "spending plan" with the $250 a month for investment included in it. Otherwise, we won't accumulate $1,000,000. Even if we don't have 33 years, our $250 could grow to a significant sum. We cut things we don't need or buy for less.

A Spending Plan is just a way to set priorities for our regular spending. During our working lives, we earn about $1.5 to $2.5 million before taxes. We can accumulate another million dollars to accomplish all that we want to do in life by using just 10 percent of that income to buy assets that "grow by themselves."

Using a Spending Plan is **like brushing your teeth**—it's a habit that isn't that difficult to learn—then it is automatic. If we want our plan to become a habit, we have to practice it. If we consciously spend our income on those items on our priority list, we can't fail to develop the habit. We are teaching ourselves that we can have whatever we want in time. We are not saying "no" to that desire. We are saying put it on our list. We will get what we want eventually.

First, our Spending Plan must include what we need to function. Our future is part of our immediate needs in the sense that if we don't prepare now, we won't have the future we want. Again, building a $1,000,000 **Wealth Reserve**™ is a lifelong process and requires making a commitment. Like building a business, it takes planning and following the steps we talked about so far.

There are a number of ways to identify the $250 a month we need to build our future. Some clients include the $250 in their automatic bill payment or have the trustee debit their account automatically. The contribution is just another bill like rent, mortgage, utilities, car payment, cable, phone, etc. They live on the balance of their income.

Others set up family goals and decide to put a certain amount in a separate account for each goal. In this way, they keep the wealth building process in the forefront of their monthly bill payments ritual. Others use their **tax refund**.

Whatever way works for you. The important part is changing the status of wealth building from a vague future to a monthly priority. Use wasted spending money to build wealth.

Most clients find that the easiest way is to set up an automatic debit of their checking account by the trustee at the time of the application for the Roth IRA. If we are using a Roth 401k or other employer account, we set up the retirement account with automatic contributions.

The Spending Plan idea works for all types of goals: college fund, emergency fund, vacation fund, new car fund, business start-up fund, whatever we decide to put at the top of our list of priorities. If we don't have this list, we can make one easily.

Clients who are successful have made written plans in some form or other. They have some idea of how much they will need at some time in the future. For short-term goals we can use our savings account but for long-term goals we need to use higher return securities. Many clients have trouble deciding which investment to use for each goal.

I explain the chart we displayed on page 12 above. Stock mutual funds are the investment of choice for any long-term accumulation goal. As per the chart, annual returns of 10-12% are the norm for any accumulation over 10-15 years. Once we build up a sizable balance in a long-term account, we can "borrow" from ourselves for short-term needs as long as we pay ourselves back.

Thus, clients have used their long-term accumulation **Wealth Reserve**™ for vacations, cars, appliances, emergencies, etc. This works if they pay themselves back. The **Wealth Reserve**™ is set up as a Roth IRA so the *contributions* are not taxed when used before age 59.5. After that age, there are no taxes at all—NEVER. However, to meet our long-term goals, we have to pay ourselves back quickly.

Another benefit of using a Spending Plan is that we become focused on how we spend our money. We are more inclined to buy only what we need. For most of us, when we can shop for groceries, we seek to get the most for our money by shopping for discounts and by buying in bulk. In the last ten years, the financial services industry has started to offer better values on products. We can avoid overpaying the middle people and buying products we really don't need.

How do we know? The *Insiders Guides* provide an easy way to save $3,000 or more on financial products we already use. There are buyer's guides for each specific area. We review some of the ways to find $250 in savings in the next chapter.

We can't build wealth by spending more than we earn. Building wealth takes patience and commitment to investing every month. Some people don't try to be disciplined investors. They let the trustee debit the $250 every month so they can't fail to invest.

Your future happiness is important too.

You are paying too much

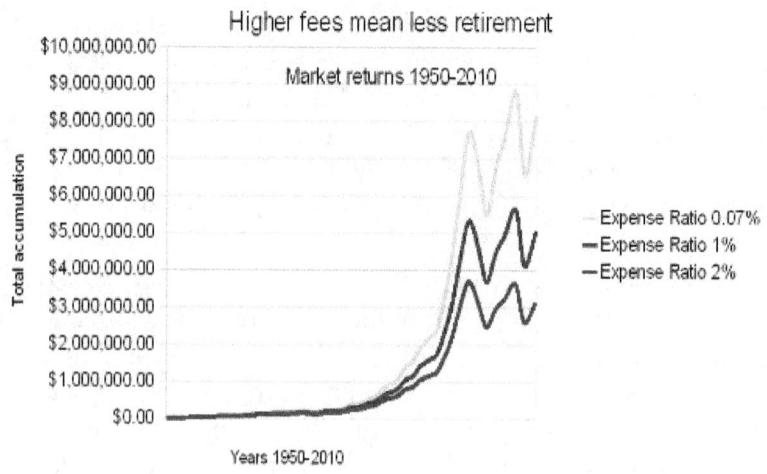

8

Use low-cost services only

It is easy to build wealth if we already have a pile of money. It takes 7-10 years to accumulate $1 million if you already have $500,000. But how do we capture that first $500,000, that first $250,000, or even that first $50,000? It comes from buying assets that 'grow by themselves.' It takes time and the easiest way to make sure we reach our goal is to make our monthly contributions automatic.

But where do we get the $250 a month? The best way is to "REDIRECT" the **cash we already spend** on things we really don't need or can buy for less.

Monthly	Accumulation at 12% per year									
	5	10	15	20	25	30	35	40	45	50
$100	$8,167	$23,004	$49,958	$98,925	$187,884	$349,496	$643,095	$1,176,477	$2,145,469	$3,905,834
$200	$16,334	$46,008	$99,916	$197,850	$375,768	$698,992	$1,286,190	$2,352,954	$4,290,938	$7,811,668
$300	$24,501	$69,012	$149,874	$296,775	$563,652	$1,048,488	$1,929,285	$3,529,431	$6,436,408	$11,717,502
$500	$40,835	$115,020	$249,790	$494,625	$939,420	$1,747,480	$3,215,475	$5,882,385	$10,727,346	$19,529,169

While working with clients, I have found that most of us waste $3,000 or more each year on financial services. We can stop paying for services we don't need. This takes a little thought and questioning on our part, but in reality it is the same process as buying any commodity. When we buy groceries, do we buy the house brand or the one on sale or the one we see advertised? On a little bigger scale, do we buy the new car advertised with a new "push" starter as opposed to an old key-type ignition? Do we pay an extra $1000 to buy the one with a screen to tell us where to go or just buy a map? The difference between paying full price for a new car and a 3 year old model with fewer gadgets can be 40%. When we put our future on top of our priority list, we can REDIRECT the savings to our long-term goals.

It is the same with financial services. Most of us are not used to shopping for insurance, mutual funds, banking and mortgages. So we don't. We are operating under the mythology of Wall Street —'professionals' say we need them to help guide us, for a price. But we don't need them anymore. The world has changed.

Let's take some examples of **annual savings**:

Auto insurance: save $400 or more EVERY year by changing/dropping some benefits we don't need.

Home insurance: save $200 or more EVERY year by changing one limit.

Life insurance: save $1,000 or more EVERY year by using direct to consumer insurer.

Mutual funds: save $2-3,000 EVERY year by using low-cost providers.

Bank: save $120 EVERY year by using a low-cost provider of the benefits we usually use.

Mortgage: save $2,000 on closings and lower interest rates.

Investments: earn 15-30% guaranteed just by paying off credit cards.

Tax refund: average refund was about $3,000 a year.

Using the Insiders' Guides put together by Dan Keppel in his book *The Insiders' Guides to Buying Discount Financial Services: Buy Direct and Save $3,000 Every Year,* we can REDIRECT the $250 a month without having to give up anything. We don't need to tighten our belt or make a budget. We can give up things we would not benefit from anyway.

Dan gave me a number of comments from people who have told him about their experience using the *Guides*.

George B. New York:
"I saved $1,356 on my vehicle insurance using your Insider's Guide to Vehicle Insurance. I saved by using some of your Insiders' 'tricks of the trade' like dropping the extras that I already had."

John D. New York:
"I canceled my life insurance and used the money to buy the mutual funds. You were right. I didn't need the insurance anymore. My kids are all grown. My new wife and I invest as much as we can now. Your Guide to 'Living' Insurance is a great way to look at our insurance needs."

Mark K. Ohio:
"I had no idea how to invest in the 401k that my new job offered. I have not been disappointed with the mutual funds suggested by other members. I saved about a $1,000 by transferring my old 401k mutual funds to the low-cost funds in your Guide. When I sold my primary residence in 2004, I followed members' advice with the gains. I use all your Guides to help me save more for my retirement since I got a late start. Thanks."

Dan has a great example of the big savings we can expect by shopping for life insurance. Dan found that people usually pick name brands instead of shopping for services they need. Companies spend a lot for TV advertising and gimmicks.

Example:

MetLife charged $983 for a $300,000 30-year **term policy**. This same $300,000 benefit was sold by Savings Bank Life Insurance for $384 a year. Their financial strength ratings are A+ and their underwriting requirements are the same. The difference, $599, over 30 years is $17,970. If invested, this difference can add $175,000 to OUR **Wealth Reserve**™ not MetLife's.

Most people are amazed at the difference a little research and shopping can accomplish. Even if we did not have Dan's *Guide*, a search of the Internet would reveal several portals that quote rates. Unfortunately, most people don't take the time to shop or don't know exactly what they need. The *Guides* help us make the decision of where to shop and what to buy.

Buying only what we need in every financial service area will provide the cash for contributions. **We give up nothing and gain our future**. Taking the time to shop in each area of our expenses helps us make our future happen. Shopping for an hour can add $175,000 to our account. Yes, it is worth it!

That is how *our low-cost tax-FREE account* works and we don't have to give up anything.

The Roth IRA Rules

Contributions:

$5,500 ($6,500 over age 50) each year
Income under $132,000 (2016) single
married $194,000 (2016)

Distributions:

Tax-FREE for contributions.
And Tax-FREE for earnings if
Over age 591/2,
Account open 5 years,
Taxable earnings unless
Disabled,
First home ($10,000),
Death

Bonus:

Account can grow tax-FREE for life
Minimum distribution rules don't apply
Heirs don't pay income tax
Account has no maximum

Check with your tax preparer
https://www.irs.gov/publications/p590a/index.html

9

Don't touch it: Let your money compound

"We continue to make more money when *snoring*
than when active."
Warren Buffett, Berkshirehathaway.com/

This is the advice of the most successful investor of our day. He is making it clear that we should NOT touch our investments very often. Contrary to the advice of the Wall Street 'professionals,' he leaves his assets alone to compound over time. He does not follow the 'hot' investment of the day. He buys the stock of growing companies around the world. He has held some investments for over 40 years.

Our emotions tell us to sell when our account balance goes down. We want to buy the next big "thing" to make up for previous losses. This is why we have a hard time following Buffett's advice. However, the emotions that cause us to be bad investors are what we can control—not the stock price of growing companies.

Our contributions to our **Wealth Reserve**™ need to be automatic so we buy more shares when the market is down and less when it is up. This helps us control our emotions. When the market is down, we need to look at the line graph on page 16. We don't know when the market will be up or down but we see that if we sell, we may miss the next advance. This is why we have to remember Warren Buffett's advice and hold on to stocks. In fact, Mr Buffett says **"our favorite holding period is forever."** http://www.berkshirehathaway.com/letters/1988.html

When we own a broad cross-section of the market, we really don't have to worry about buying and selling our mutual funds. There is no better investment for the long term. Besides, what would we buy if we sold? We have seen that stocks are the safest investment for periods over 10 years.

We have learned that the only way to avoid bad investment decisions is to NOT make any investment decisions in haste. Stick with the idea that we only have to look at our tax-FREE account once a year. At that time, I make sure I am making contributions to the specific mutual fund I need to build in order to keep them equally funded.

For instance, when I first started investing, I used the 500 Index. After I had accumulated enough to buy the Extended Market Index, I sold shares of 500 Index ($3,000) and bought it. I kept investing into the 500 Index until I had the minimum for the next one on the list. I repeated this pattern until I had the minimum in each. Then I picked one to add $250 a month for one year. The next year, I did the same until I completed the list again and again.

Today, I am still making contributions using the same rotation. Once a year, I compare the total account balance to where I think it should be. I note what happened during the year for any one fund. I go to the Vanguard site and read about that fund. Do I need to make a change? No, usually I don't. I only use the 10 funds listed above. They have consistently done well over the years.

Notice that when we buy each fund at first, we have to sell shares in the 500 Index to do so. Because we are using a Roth IRA, there is no tax on this sale if the share price has gone up. Also, each year, our dividends are re-invested without paying tax on that income. This is part of the **miracle of compounding**. Our account is growing without taxes each year. Any other non-retirement account would be diminished by the tax paid each year.

There is no need to sell funds that have done well in order to re-balance the 10 funds' balances equally. Most of the research shows that re-balancing each year does not change the long-term outcome of the whole portfolio. Some clients use their contributions each year to add to the fund that has grown the least. However, as each fund becomes larger, the effect of adding contributions becomes smaller over time.

When we have to sell shares to meet an emergency or avoid interest payments by using cash for large ticket items, we may sell shares in each fund by equal dollar amounts. This is a better strategy than selling shares in only one fund since we don't know which fund may recover the fastest going forward. In the same way as accumulating shares, we need to reimburse our account for the amount used. It is very desirable to also continue to make contributions at the regular rate--$250 per month. This way we are assured of catching up to our position as we reach our goal.

However, we found that after accumulating a large proportion of our goal, adding the $250 per month did not seem to matter to the outcome. For instance, our client whose account is shown on page 24 took $25,000 for a used luxury car in the year the account hit over half a million. He also stopped making contributions. His account total did not suffer long term.

Actually this client redirected his $250 monthly contribution to his grandchild's **Wealth Reserve**™ so that they might have a financial foundation all their life. If he keeps giving this $3,000 a year to his offspring for 35 years, they could have $1,000,000 by age 50. The grandchild "earns" $3,000 a year doing odd jobs for him. Learn more about this "Gift of a Lifetime" in Dan Keppel's book, amazon.com/Give-your-Grandchild-000-Lifetime/.

Our tax-FREE account does not require us to hire an advisor to manage it. Advisors do not know what the future holds anymore than we do so paying them 2-3% each year just reduces our annual returns. Their fees/charges can take up to 63% of our total accumulations over time. We are investing for the long term and there is no proof that switching from one fund to another during the year does anything to help our results. As we add more contributions, we can rotate through each fund we use. The less we tamper with our fund balances the better our experience will be. That is how *our low-cost tax-FREE account* works.

Remember Mr Buffett's strategy:

"our favorite holding period is forever."

Learn Your Biases

Action bias: Wall Street tells us the "buy and hold" strategy is wrong.

Beginner's luck bias: My first stock pick was genius. I'm an intuitive trader.

Optimism bias: I made money the last time I picked a stock. I can do it again.

Overconfidence: I can beat the market despite the odds 9:1 against.
    "Nearly two-thirds rated their financial sophistication as advanced."

Sunk cost fallacy: I can't sell my losers now—I will wait till they recover.

Loss aversion bias: I hate losing my small nest egg so I use bonds not stocks.

House money bias: I can afford to take more risk with my big 'paper' gains.

Lottery bias: You got to be in it to win it and it might as well be me this time.

Hindsight: Tendency to rewrite our own history to make ourselves look good.

Base rate bias: I sold because the market fell already and will fall again.

Statistical error: I have lost 5 times, the odds are now in my favor.

Herding: Every one else is selling. "Be fearful when others are greedy."

Anchoring: Great stock I want went from $90 to $50 makes it a bargain.

Choice under conflict: I can't decide when two or more attractive options.

Regret aversion: I can't decide when I fear I might make the wrong choice.

Attribution bias: errors in analysis of cause of situation especially blame.

Confirmation bias: finding unwarranted justifications for past behavior.

Endowment effect: ascribe more value to things merely because I own them.

Status quo bias: any change from my current situation is perceived as a loss.

More: http://www.amazon.com/Why-Smart-People-Make-Money-Mistakes-Correct/dp/0684859386

10

Tax-FREE income

We have used the 10 funds to build wealth. We have learned to be patient and accumulate $1,000,000 or more. We have paid back any amounts that we borrowed to pay cash for large purchases. We have been fortunate that the historical averages of market returns have produced the accumulations we set as our goals.

NOW WHAT?

Now we can take $80,000 out of the account each year and pay no income taxes. As of 2015, most states follow the IRS code on our **Wealth Reserve**™, a Roth IRA—§ 408 trust account.
http://www.irs.gov/retirement/article/0,,id=137307,00.html

Some clients have moved some of their accumulations into a bond fund in order to provide a monthly check to their checking account for their regular expenses. They created a retirement spending plan that assured them of that monthly income of a fixed dollar amount with this Guide. amazon.com/Your-Retirement-Spending-Plan-enough

We have to create our $1,000,000 nest egg in order to provide the same buying power as we have today because of inflation. I am assuming that most families will need at least $50,000 a year to live on in retirement. We don't know what will happen to Social Security by 2033. We don't know what employer pensions might look like by then. I am assuming that inflation will continue at a 3% rate. It might be more or less. I have no idea. However, we must prepare for inflation.

At 3%, inflation will make the goods we buy now for $50,000 cost about $80,000. This is not exact. I don't know what will happen in 30 days let alone 30 years. If Social Security or employer pensions can add to our basic income, that is fine. But we don't want to count on them.

I am using $50,000 as a basic needs income because that has been my experience of what working people desire. It is also an amount that could be generated by our $1,000,000 account balance. Many clients use 6-8% as a target for their investment returns in retirement. This is just an approximation of the average returns over time.

Some clients move half their balances into a bond or balanced fund in order to generate the income for the coming year. The balance of their account remains in the broad stock funds we have listed above. These funds will continue to produce returns in the 10-12% range. If there is a bad year like 2008, we are not taking money out of our principal at a bad time. We take the money from a bond fund like the Vanguard Total Bond which has traditionally been less volatile.

The funds we have listed above include some of the most consistent low volatility returns over time. The *Wellesley Income* fund has produced over 10% per year on average since 1970. It lost 10% when the market fell 40% in 2008. **This fund alone might be our source** of annual withdrawals of principal and dividends. Since this account is not taxable, there are no tax considerations in the decision of which fund to tap for our monthly income.

Because we have no tax liability on this income of $80,000 per year, we may not have to pay tax on our other income like Social Security and/or our qualified retirement funds. 85% of Social Security benefits are currently subject to federal income taxes. The IRS worksheet determines the percentage based on all our other income. Typically those with little or no other income currently have no tax due on their Social Security benefits. Pensions are taxed as income since we did not pay tax on the contributions.

In most cases, we will pay little income tax on our income in retirement since the bulk of it, $80,000 ($50,000 adjusted for inflation), will be tax-FREE. This will give us up to 30% or more cash to spend compared with others who do not have the **Wealth Reserve**™. Pensions and other taxable income may be taxed at even higher rates in the future to pay for the two wars and two tax cuts that we endured since 2001. We have never gone to war and taken tax breaks at the same time before so this will take time to work out.

Our tax-FREE income will provide us with our basic-needs income and if we continue to follow the same 10 steps of building wealth, we will find a comfortable lifestyle throughout the 30 to 40 years of not working unless we want to.

I and many clients are assuming we will work at least part time after we take full retirement and begin collecting Social Security. If benefits are cut, we will need to work. We are encouraged to use our tax-FREE income to develop a small business since this can help us control the income that is taxed.

As I mentioned at the beginning of this book, many working millionaires are self-employed. Running a small business is a great way to control the taxes they pay. Taxes are the biggest killer of wealth building that exists. It destroys the compounding factor.

The accumulation of $1,000,000 over time can be achieved with patience and perseverance. Spending the income that $1,000,000 can generate may require us to take some principal from time to time. If we use the same 10 steps of wealth building to do this, we will probably have enough to take care of long-term health care and other unforeseen expenses. Since we don't know what may happen, we will want to continue the same habits we have developed before retirement. We live within our means.

We may find that we will have a sizable legacy as we age. There are many ways to pass on our wealth that don't require attorney's fees or complicated legal formulations. Many clients have found that incremental gifts to charity and family provide immediate gratification. They have used the suggestions for wealth transfer Dan Keppel presented in the *Retirement Spending Plan*.

This retirement income is tax-FREE and has the purchasing power of about $50,000 in today's dollars. Working millionaires typically don't go out and buy a mansion and the trappings of the wealthy when they retire. They usually have paid off their homes. They travel and share with family. Some continue to earn income doing what they enjoy or provide help to others in their volunteer efforts. That is how *our low-cost tax-FREE account* works.

We gain more by paying fewer fees and no taxes.

How to Buy Securities for Retirement

1. Cost matters: Broker/advisor cost 1% to 3%

If you use a salesperson, fees can cost HALF A NEST EGG!
$3,000 per year @11% for 40 years = $2,169,740
$3,000 per year @11-1% for 40 years = $1,594,195
$3,000 per year @11-2% for 40 years = $1,179,107
$3,000 per year @11-3% for 40 years = $878,570

2. Broker/advisor stock picking does not beat index funds over the long run. No money manager has been able to beat the market consistently. No one can forecast the future. Insider trading is illegal except for Congresspeople. http://www.reuters.com/article/markets-saft-idUSL2N14V2OV20160113

3. Time is the key to investment success. The chance of you buying AND selling, both, at the right times, is near zero.

4. A Tax-FREE investment account increases your balance 25%.

5. Putting all your money in one stock or market sector guarantees failure over time. No one investment is perfect.

6. 'Dollar cost average' buying technique lowers the cost of shares over time. When you invest a fixed amount each month, you buy more mutual fund shares when the price is low and less when high. Over time, you will own more shares at a lower average cost.

7. That is low-cost—the best predictor of investment success.

The wealthy control their biases

We can learn to control our biases. We learn that acting on hunches does not work for investing. The market is NOT a roulette wheel. It is a "device for transferring money from the **impatient to the patient**." Tom was patient even with "losses" on page 24.

We don't have to settle for 3.79% returns on our money. We learn the odds are with us if we *stay pat*. Compounding, not trading is the key to success. To compound, we must NOT follow the herd. We must remember that we can't get rich by "playing" the game— only the house makes money then. Wall Street creates stories of riches to get us to give them money. Then they take it: No refunds.

Low-cost stock index funds earn 10-12% over the long term. Our money doubles every 6-7 years. We understand we will lose money "on paper" some years just like a business. However, our INVESTMENT ATTITUDE is all business and we act as an owner. In fact, we buy more shares when prices are low. We realize that we will never be in the NBA of investors so why kid ourselves. We smile when others brag about their quick profits. It's B.S. We know that no one makes a killing without insider info.

No matter what our investment goals or portfolio allocation, we earn more when we pay less. Vanguard is owned by its investors and it employs the same qualified advisors as we use now but on salary, not on high commissions and fees. Vanguard has no incentive to gouge or mislead us.

Forget Wall Street. They have taken our earnings long enough. They have lobbied Congress with $3.4 billion to keep the system producing their $560 billion annual paydays and bonuses.

As you take steps to build your wealth and accumulate for your future, you might need help. You might need to know if this or that fund can provide you with a balanced asset portfolio or a less aggressive glide path. You realize your broker cannot find the next Apple stock and you don't want to chase yield. You agree that some Vanguard funds can help you reach your goals.

Vanguard has been attracting more of us who see how Wall Street's fees can take up to 63% of our potential nest egg. The industry has made building wealth a mystery so that they could tell us we need them: a "doctor" of financial health who we pay very well. The industry takes $560 billions from investors' accounts year after year with negative improvement—3.79% vs 11%. Trading stocks does NOT benefit us.

A person paying 2-3% of their nest egg every year to an advisor can't then admit they get very little for their money. Most advisors can't beat the investment return of the market so that $3,000-$5,000 a year in fees is really paying for Wall Street hype. Over time that fee goes up as our balance goes up and can take up to 63% of our total possible accumulations. Advisors like to buy and sell securities creating taxes and fees that don't help us.

As Buffett said, **compounding is key** to reaching our money goals. If we pay 2% to get 10-12%, we net 8-10%. We know that no advisor can guarantee 10-12%! Most studies show investing directly without a "professional" can yield a better result; there is no reason to give up 2%. Advisors usually charge 2-3% whether they beat the averages or not so it is better to go for the 10-12% on our own. **Advisors don't give refunds**!
https://www.ispot.tv/ad/AwfU/charles-schwab-father-and-son

The clear winning strategy is to use low-cost funds and let compounding work its magic. Over time using a tax-FREE account without an advisor fee, we can accumulate $1,000,000 from $250 a month at 10-12%. Using a compounding calculator http://www.moneychimp.com/calculator/compound_interest_calculator.htm, we find the range is 32 to 36 years. If we and our spouse each have an account, we can shorten the time to 26-29 years.

If we use an advisor, we may give up over $400,000 in total accumulation. Costs include lower earnings and market timing mistakes and bad investments. Research has shown that the average brokerage investor actually earns about **3.79%** annually. **Great for them; bad for us!**

Our 10 funds for building wealth are successful because they are straightforward strategies inside a unique **tax-FREE low-cost IRS account** that eliminates the biggest killer of wealth: TAXES. We have seen that **compounding** over time is the *real engine* for building wealth. Most people are NOT going to be successful at this because they have no patience to let compounding do the work. Compounding only works if we leave our funds alone.

We can be our own masters of tax-FREE wealth with patience.

There is no need to pick stocks or hire expensive advisors or product pushers with hidden fees. We can do it ourselves as long as we have a plan. Our plan is on page 11.

You must take the first step. I don't sell products so I won't be calling you. You have to call Vanguard or TIAA *yourself* to set up your account. Advisors can't. It takes about an hour to set up a Roth IRA for both of you with a telephone rep. You can begin with TIAA and $100 automatic contributions or Vanguard with $1,000. Put the contributions on automatic so you don't have to decide every month whether to invest. That is usually how people fail. Life happens and there is always an emergency that requires cash. But future life happens too and you want to be spending your $80,000 not praying Washington won't cut Social Security benefits every year.

There is a clear reason why "working millionaires" become wealthy. It is not luck or inheritance. Millions of immigrants to this country have done it before. They lived below their means. They saved and invested in businesses they worked. They did not let temporary cash flow problems stop them from building wealth. They used the same path to building wealth every day.

As many clients say, "I never even miss the contributions because I never see them. Then all of a sudden, I see my statement has $25,000, $50,000, $250,000, $1,000,000. We are talking real money here."

Wealth comes from your *Investment Attitude*.

Call Vanguard **800 319-4254**
https://personal.vanguard.com/us/openaccount

or TIAA **844 842-2472** today.
https://publictools.tiaa-cref.org/public/authentication/ira/getstarted

Questions?

IANBooksEditor@yahoo.com

The Author

Law Steeple has been in financial services for over 20 years. He was a managing executive of the sales units of a number of bank securities firms. He is one of the insiders who contributed to the The Insiders Guides set of buyers' guides edited by Dan Keppel. The guides provide specific ways to save on all financial services. ***The Insiders' Guides to Buying Discount Financial Services: Buy Direct and Save $3,000 Every Year*** is available at Amazon, Barnes and Noble, Abebooks. Law lives in New Jersey and Florida.

To receive Dan Keppel's weekly Alert, go to www.TheInsidersGuides.com